About
Skill Builders
Multiplication

by R. B. Snow

Welcome to RBP Books' Skill Builders series. Like our Summer Bridge Activities collection, the Skill Builders series is designed to make learning both fun and rewarding.

Skill Builders 3rd Grade Multiplication provides students with focused practice to help reinforce and develop multiplication skills. Each Skill Builders volume is grade-level appropriate with clear examples and instructions to guide each lesson. In accordance with NCTM standards, exercises include a variety of activities to help students develop their ability to multiply numbers.

A critical thinking section includes exercises to develop higher-order thinking skills.

Learning is more effective when approached with an element of fun and enthusiasm—just as most children approach life. That's why the Skill Builders combine entertaining and academically sound exercises and fun themes to make reviewing basic skills fun and effective, for both you and your budding scholars.

Table of Contents

Problem Solving

Solve the problems below using the illustrations to create the problem and answer. An example is done for you.

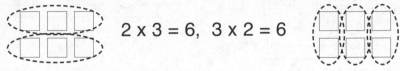

$2 \times 3 = 6, \ 3 \times 2 = 6$

1. ⚪⚪⚪⚪
   ⚪⚪⚪⚪ ___ x ___ = ___, ___ x ___ = ___ ⚪⚪⚪⚪
   ⚪⚪⚪⚪

2. △△△△△△
   △△△△△△ ___ x ___ = ___, ___ x ___ = ___ △△△△△△
   △△△△△△

3. ▫▫▫▫
   ▫▫▫▫ ___ x ___ = ___, ___ x ___ = ___ ▫▫▫▫
   ▫▫▫▫

4. ⚪⚪⚪⚪⚪
   ⚪⚪⚪⚪⚪ ___ x ___ = ___, ___ x ___ = ___ ⚪⚪⚪⚪⚪
   ⚪⚪⚪⚪⚪

5. △△△△△
   △△△△△ ___ x ___ = ___, ___ x ___ = ___ △△△△△
   △△△△△

6. ▫▫▫▫▫▫
   ▫▫▫▫▫▫ ___ x ___ = ___, ___ x ___ = ___ ▫▫▫▫▫▫
   ▫▫▫▫▫▫

Solve the problems.

> Any number multiplied by 1 equals that number.

> Any number multiplied by 0 equals 0.

1. 0 x 1 = __**0**__

0 x 2 = _____

0 x 3 = _____

0 x 4 = _____

0 x 5 = _____

0 x 6 = _____

0 x 7 = _____

0 x 8 = _____

0 x 9 = _____

2. 1 x 1 = __**1**__

1 x 2 = _____

1 x 3 = _____

1 x 4 = _____

1 x 5 = _____

1 x 6 = _____

1 x 7 = _____

1 x 8 = _____

1 x 9 = _____

3. 2 x 1 = __**2**__

2 x 2 = _____

2 x 3 = _____

2 x 4 = _____

2 x 5 = _____

2 x 6 = _____

2 x 7 = _____

2 x 8 = _____

2 x 9 = _____

Two | Four | Six | Eight

> Who do we appreciate? Multiples! Yeah!

Fill in the tables.

5. 4 x 1 = ___**4**___
4 x 2 = _____
4 x 3 = _____
4 x 4 = _____
4 x 5 = _____
4 x 6 = _____
4 x 7 = _____
4 x 8 = _____
4 x 9 = _____

4. 3 x 1 = ___**3**___
3 x 2 = _____
3 x 3 = _____
3 x 4 = _____
3 x 5 = _____
3 x 6 = _____
3 x 7 = _____
3 x 8 = _____
3 x 9 = _____

6. 5 x 1 = ___**5**___
5 x 2 = _____
5 x 3 = _____
5 x 4 = _____
5 x 5 = _____
5 x 6 = _____
5 x 7 = _____
5 x 8 = _____
5 x 9 = _____

Draw a line from the multiplication problem to the correct picture.

1.   3 x 2

2.   2 x 5

3.   4 x 2

4.   3 x 4

5.   4 x 5

6.   5 x 5

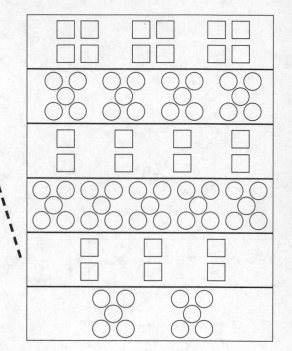

Draw pictures to show the problems.

7.   4 x 4

8.   3 x 3

9.   2 x 5

10.   4 x 1

Fill in the tables.

1. 6 x 1 = **6**
  6 x 2 = _____
  6 x 3 = _____
  6 x 4 = _____
  6 x 5 = _____
  6 x 6 = _____
  6 x 7 = _____
  6 x 8 = _____
  6 x 9 = _____

2. 7 x 1 = **7**
  7 x 2 = _____
  7 x 3 = _____
  7 x 4 = _____
  7 x 5 = _____
  7 x 6 = _____
  7 x 7 = _____
  7 x 8 = _____
  7 x 9 = _____

3. 8 x 1 = **8**
  8 x 2 = _____
  8 x 3 = _____
  8 x 4 = _____
  8 x 5 = _____
  8 x 6 = _____
  8 x 7 = _____
  8 x 8 = _____
  8 x 9 = _____

4. 9 x 1 = **9**
  9 x 2 = _____
  9 x 3 = _____
  9 x 4 = _____
  9 x 5 = _____
  9 x 6 = _____
  9 x 7 = _____
  9 x 8 = _____
  9 x 9 = _____

Multiplication Grade 3—RBP3764

Relate these facts to complete the sequence.

1. $2 \times 4 = \underline{\textbf{8}}$ so $4 \times 2 = \underline{\textbf{8}}$

2. $5 \times 3 = \underline{\hphantom{00}}$ so $3 \times 5 = \underline{\hphantom{00}}$

3. $1 \times 6 = \underline{\hphantom{00}}$ so $6 \times 1 = \underline{\hphantom{00}}$

4. $2 \times 5 = \underline{\hphantom{00}}$ so $5 \times 2 = \underline{\hphantom{00}}$

5. $7 \times 3 = \underline{\hphantom{00}}$ so $3 \times 7 = \underline{\hphantom{00}}$

6. $3 \times 4 = \underline{\hphantom{00}}$ so $4 \times 3 = \underline{\hphantom{00}}$

7. $2 \times 9 = \underline{\hphantom{00}}$ so $9 \times 2 = \underline{\hphantom{00}}$

8. $4 \times 6 = \underline{\hphantom{00}}$ so $6 \times 4 = \underline{\hphantom{00}}$

9. $2 \times 7 = \underline{\hphantom{00}}$ so $7 \times 2 = \underline{\hphantom{00}}$

10. $2 \times 3 = \underline{\hphantom{00}}$ so $3 \times 2 = \underline{\hphantom{00}}$

11. $8 \times 2 = \underline{\hphantom{00}}$ so $2 \times 8 = \underline{\hphantom{00}}$

12. $9 \times 4 = \underline{\hphantom{00}}$ so $4 \times 9 = \underline{\hphantom{00}}$

Complete the chart; then answer the questions.

x	1	2	3	4	5	6	7	8	9
1									
2									
3									
4									
5									
6									
7									
8									
9									

1. What does any number times 1 equal? _____
2. What pattern do you see in the 2s? _____
3. What pattern do you see in the 5s? _____
4. Add the digits for each answer in the 9s. What do they equal? _____
5. 3 x 4 = 12. What does 4 x 3 equal? _____

Multiplication Practice: 1–9

Solve each problem.

1.
$$\begin{array}{r} 2 \\ \times\ 2 \\ \hline \mathbf{4} \end{array}\qquad \begin{array}{r} 3 \\ \times\ 2 \\ \hline \end{array}\qquad \begin{array}{r} 5 \\ \times\ 3 \\ \hline \end{array}\qquad \begin{array}{r} 1 \\ \times\ 6 \\ \hline \end{array}\qquad \begin{array}{r} 6 \\ \times\ 2 \\ \hline \end{array}$$

2.
$$\begin{array}{r} 2 \\ \times\ 8 \\ \hline \end{array}\qquad \begin{array}{r} 5 \\ \times\ 2 \\ \hline \end{array}\qquad \begin{array}{r} 2 \\ \times\ 6 \\ \hline \end{array}\qquad \begin{array}{r} 2 \\ \times\ 4 \\ \hline \end{array}\qquad \begin{array}{r} 2 \\ \times\ 1 \\ \hline \end{array}$$

3.
$$\begin{array}{r} 7 \\ \times\ 2 \\ \hline \end{array}\qquad \begin{array}{r} 3 \\ \times\ 6 \\ \hline \end{array}\qquad \begin{array}{r} 9 \\ \times\ 2 \\ \hline \end{array}\qquad \begin{array}{r} 8 \\ \times\ 2 \\ \hline \end{array}\qquad \begin{array}{r} 4 \\ \times\ 5 \\ \hline \end{array}$$

4.
$$\begin{array}{r} 3 \\ \times\ 9 \\ \hline \end{array}\qquad \begin{array}{r} 6 \\ \times\ 5 \\ \hline \end{array}\qquad \begin{array}{r} 4 \\ \times\ 6 \\ \hline \end{array}\qquad \begin{array}{r} 3 \\ \times\ 7 \\ \hline \end{array}\qquad \begin{array}{r} 8 \\ \times\ 3 \\ \hline \end{array}$$

5.
$$\begin{array}{r} 4 \\ \times\ 4 \\ \hline \end{array}\qquad \begin{array}{r} 5 \\ \times\ 6 \\ \hline \end{array}\qquad \begin{array}{r} 5 \\ \times\ 8 \\ \hline \end{array}\qquad \begin{array}{r} 7 \\ \times\ 9 \\ \hline \end{array}\qquad \begin{array}{r} 8 \\ \times\ 8 \\ \hline \end{array}$$

Read and solve the problems. Show your work in the box.
Write your answer on the line.

1.

Randy had 6 bags.

He put 9 marbles in each bag.

How many marbles did
he have in all?

```
  6
x 9
54
```

He has 54 marbles.

2.

Stan has 4 stacks of cards
with 8 cards in each stack.

How many cards does
he have?

_____

3.

Jennifer jumped over 5 rocks.

She jumped over each rock
9 times.

How many times did
she jump?

_____

4.

Zach runs 6 miles, 5 days
a week.

How many miles does he
run each week?

_____

5.

The skaters skated in 7 groups
with 4 in each group.

How many skaters were there
in all?

_____

I bet you can do
this exercise
in a snap!

Greater Than and Less Than

Use the >, <, or = signs to describe the relationship between the pairs.

1. 2 x 6 (<) 7 x 2   5 x 3 ( ) 4 x 4

2. 2 x 4 ( ) 6 x 1   9 x 4 ( ) 6 x 6

3. 7 x 5 ( ) 6 x 7   4 x 5 ( ) 5 x 3

4. 9 x 5 ( ) 7 x 6   6 x 7 ( ) 7 x 6

5. 8 x 4 ( ) 9 x 3   3 x 6 ( ) 4 x 5

6. 3 x 7 ( ) 5 x 5   8 x 5 ( ) 9 x 7

7. 6 x 0 ( ) 0 x 10   2 x 6 ( ) 6 + 6

8. 5 x 4 ( ) 5 x 3   9 x 1 ( ) 9 + 9

www.summerbridgeactivities.com

Fill in the charts.

1.

Multiply by 2	
9	**18**
5	
3	
6	
7	
4	
2	
8	

2.

Multiply by 5	
9	
5	
3	
6	
7	
4	
2	
8	

3.

Multiply by 3	
9	
5	
3	
6	
7	
4	
2	
8	

4.

Multiply by 6	
9	
5	
3	
6	
7	
4	
2	
8	

5.

Multiply by 9	
9	
5	
3	
6	
7	
4	
2	
8	

6.

Multiply by 4	
9	
5	
3	
6	
7	
4	
2	
8	

Multiplication Grade 3—RBP3764

Solve each problem below.

1. $6 \times 6 = \underline{\textbf{36}}$ $7 \times 5 = \underline{\hspace{1cm}}$ $9 \times 4 = \underline{\hspace{1cm}}$

      $7 \times 8 = \underline{\hspace{1cm}}$ $4 \times 7 = \underline{\hspace{1cm}}$ $5 \times 3 = \underline{\hspace{1cm}}$

2. $3 \times 7 = \underline{\hspace{1cm}}$ $9 \times 6 = \underline{\hspace{1cm}}$ $8 \times 8 = \underline{\hspace{1cm}}$

      $8 \times 5 = \underline{\hspace{1cm}}$ $8 \times 6 = \underline{\hspace{1cm}}$ $9 \times 5 = \underline{\hspace{1cm}}$

3. $4 \times 4 = \underline{\hspace{1cm}}$ $6 \times 7 = \underline{\hspace{1cm}}$ $8 \times 4 = \underline{\hspace{1cm}}$

      $3 \times 9 = \underline{\hspace{1cm}}$ $6 \times 5 = \underline{\hspace{1cm}}$ $4 \times 8 = \underline{\hspace{1cm}}$

4. $7 \times 6 = \underline{\hspace{1cm}}$ $9 \times 8 = \underline{\hspace{1cm}}$ $7 \times 7 = \underline{\hspace{1cm}}$

      $5 \times 7 = \underline{\hspace{1cm}}$ $5 \times 5 = \underline{\hspace{1cm}}$ $8 \times 6 = \underline{\hspace{1cm}}$

5. $3 \times 6 = \underline{\hspace{1cm}}$ $6 \times 8 = \underline{\hspace{1cm}}$ $9 \times 7 = \underline{\hspace{1cm}}$

      $6 \times 9 = \underline{\hspace{1cm}}$ $8 \times 9 = \underline{\hspace{1cm}}$ $7 \times 3 = \underline{\hspace{1cm}}$

Problem Solving: 0–9

Solve each problem below.

1. $5 \times 3 \times 2 =$ __**30**__ $\quad 2 \times 6 \times 1 =$ ____ $\quad 4 \times 8 \times 1 =$ ____

2. $7 \times 2 \times 2 =$ ____ $\quad 4 \times 5 \times 2 =$ ____ $\quad 3 \times 1 \times 6 =$ ____

3. $6 \times 2 \times 3 =$ ____ $\quad 3 \times 5 \times 2 =$ ____ $\quad 4 \times 3 \times 3 =$ ____

4. $7 \times 2 \times 3 =$ ____ $\quad 3 \times 2 \times 9 =$ ____ $\quad 5 \times 2 \times 6 =$ ____

5. $4 \times 2 \times 2 =$ ____ $\quad 6 \times 1 \times 3 =$ ____ $\quad 7 \times 3 \times 0 =$ ____

6. $0 \times 6 \times 9 =$ ____ $\quad 2 \times 5 \times 0 =$ ____ $\quad 1 \times 7 \times 8 =$ ____

Multiplication Grade 3—RBP3764

Fill in the tables.

1. 10 x 1 = __**10**__

10 x 2 = _____

10 x 3 = _____

10 x 4 = _____

10 x 5 = _____

10 x 6 = _____

10 x 7 = _____

10 x 8 = _____

10 x 9 = _____

2. 11 x 1 = __**11**__

11 x 2 = _____

11 x 3 = _____

11 x 4 = _____

11 x 5 = _____

11 x 6 = _____

11 x 7 = _____

11 x 8 = _____

11 x 9 = _____

3. 12 x 1 = __**12**__

12 x 2 = _____

12 x 3 = _____

12 x 4 = _____

12 x 5 = _____

12 x 6 = _____

12 x 7 = _____

12 x 8 = _____

12 x 9 = _____

Solve each problem below.

1.

10	10	10	10	10
x 8	x 3	x 6	x 2	x 0
80				

2.

10	10	10	10	10
x 5	x 7	x 4	x 9	x 1

3.

11	11	11	11	11
x 8	x 3	x 6	x 2	x 0

4.

11	11	11	11	11
x 5	x 7	x 4	x 9	x 1

5.

12	12	12	12	12
x 8	x 3	x 6	x 2	x 0

Problem Solving: 10–12

Solve each problem below.

6.	12 x 5	12 x 7	12 x 4	12 x 9	12 x 1
7.	12 x 4	11 x 2	10 x 2	10 x 3	12 x 1
8.	11 x 3	10 x 7	12 x 3	11 x 4	10 x 1
9.	12 x 2	10 x 6	11 x 5	12 x 5	10 x 8
10.	10 x 9	11 x 6	10 x 5	12 x 6	11 x 7

Practice: Missing Numbers

What is the missing number?

1.   __7__ x 11 = 77

2.   8 x 5 = _____

3.   6 x _____ = 54

4.   ____ x 9 = 36

5.   4 x _____ = 16

6.   ____ x 8 = 72

7.   12 x ____ = 144

8.   3 x _____ = 36

9.   6 x 4 = _____

10.   ___ x 11 = 44

11.   7 x _____ = 42

12.   5 x _____ = 35

Missing numbers? I'm on the case!

© RBP Books   Multiplication Grade 3—RBP3764

Multiplication Wheels

Complete each wheel below by multiplying from the center out to the edge for each area.

1.

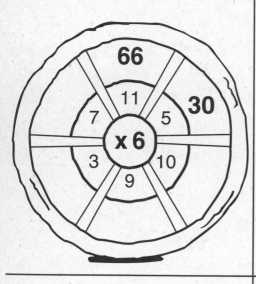

2.

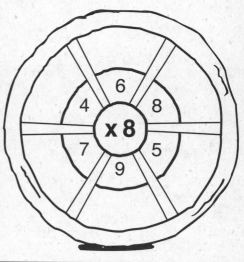

3.

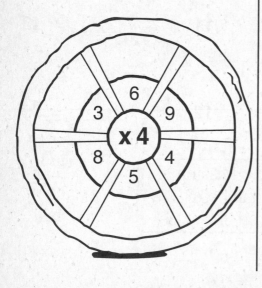

4.

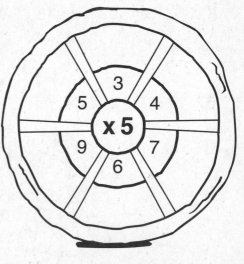

Keep on rollin' through those equations, partner!

5.

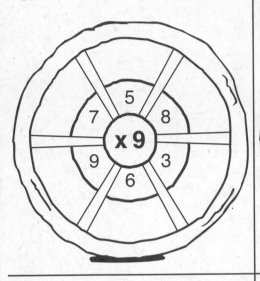

6.

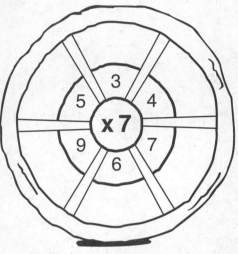

7.

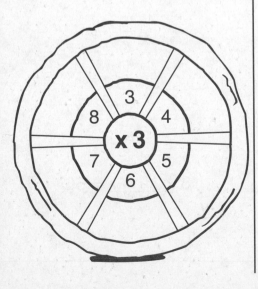

8.

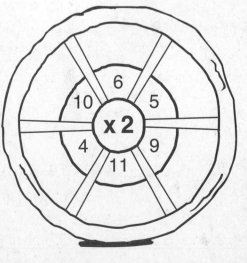

Write the correct numeral in the blanks.

1. $9 \times \underline{\textbf{1}} = 9$ $3 \times \underline{\hspace{1cm}} = 21$

2. $4 \times \underline{\hspace{1cm}} = 28$ $2 \times \underline{\hspace{1cm}} = 16$

3. $5 \times \underline{\hspace{1cm}} = 50$ $7 \times \underline{\hspace{1cm}} = 42$

4. $\underline{\hspace{1cm}} \times 4 = 36$ $\underline{\hspace{1cm}} \times 6 = 60$

5. $\underline{\hspace{1cm}} \times 8 = 48$ $\underline{\hspace{1cm}} \times 3 = 15$

6. $5 \times 4 = \underline{\hspace{1cm}}$ $6 \times 2 = \underline{\hspace{1cm}}$

7. $0 \times 5 = \underline{\hspace{1cm}}$ $\underline{\hspace{1cm}} \times 7 = 77$

8. $\underline{\hspace{1cm}} \times 2 = 14$ $8 \times \underline{\hspace{1cm}} = 56$

9. $8 \times \underline{\hspace{1cm}} = 32$ $1 \times \underline{\hspace{1cm}} = 12$

10.   10 x _____ = 0   _____ x 7 = 49

11.   _____ x 5 = 50   9 x 1 = _____

12.   3 x _____ = 30   _____ x 10 = 100

13.   3 x _____ = 27   7 x _____ = 42

14.   _____ x 7 = 84   9 x _____ = 81

15.   _____ x 5 = 45   _____ x 4 = 12

16.   _____ x 8 = 64   12 x _____ = 48

17.   5 x _____ = 55   4 x _____ = 28

18.   _____ x 8 = 72   _____ x 7 = 63

Multiplication Grade 3—RBP3764

Read and solve the problems. Show your work in the box. Write your answer on the line.

1.

Eight children went for a hike.

Each child carried a backpack with 6 bandages in it.

How many bandages do they have total?

```
    8
  x 6
   48
```

48 bandages

2.

In the evening, Zoe helps set up camp. There are 3 rows with 8 tents in each row.

How many tents are there?

_____

3.

Each car has 4 tires.

There are 9 cars.

How many tires are there altogether?

_____

4.

The iguanas eat 3 times a week.

How many times will Emmett need to feed the iguanas in the next 12 weeks?

_____

5.

Sara mows 5 lawns a week.

If she mows lawns for 11 weeks, how many lawns will she mow altogether?

_____

We love this math stuff!

2-Digit Multiplication

Solve each problem.

1.

$$\begin{array}{r} 12 \\ \times\ 4 \\ \hline \end{array}$$
$$\begin{array}{r} 11 \\ \times\ 2 \\ \hline \end{array}$$
$$\begin{array}{r} 13 \\ \times\ 2 \\ \hline \end{array}$$
$$\begin{array}{r} 13 \\ \times\ 3 \\ \hline \end{array}$$
$$\begin{array}{r} 14 \\ \times\ 1 \\ \hline \end{array}$$

2.

$$\begin{array}{r} 11 \\ \times\ 3 \\ \hline \end{array}$$
$$\begin{array}{r} 14 \\ \times\ 2 \\ \hline \end{array}$$
$$\begin{array}{r} 12 \\ \times\ 3 \\ \hline \end{array}$$
$$\begin{array}{r} 11 \\ \times\ 4 \\ \hline \end{array}$$
$$\begin{array}{r} 23 \\ \times\ 3 \\ \hline \end{array}$$

3.

$$\begin{array}{r} 13 \\ \times\ 1 \\ \hline \end{array}$$
$$\begin{array}{r} 11 \\ \times\ 6 \\ \hline \end{array}$$
$$\begin{array}{r} 22 \\ \times\ 3 \\ \hline \end{array}$$
$$\begin{array}{r} 32 \\ \times\ 2 \\ \hline \end{array}$$
$$\begin{array}{r} 44 \\ \times\ 2 \\ \hline \end{array}$$

4.

$$\begin{array}{r} 42 \\ \times\ 2 \\ \hline \end{array}$$
$$\begin{array}{r} 24 \\ \times\ 2 \\ \hline \end{array}$$
$$\begin{array}{r} 22 \\ \times\ 2 \\ \hline \end{array}$$
$$\begin{array}{r} 21 \\ \times\ 3 \\ \hline \end{array}$$
$$\begin{array}{r} 11 \\ \times\ 7 \\ \hline \end{array}$$

5.

$$\begin{array}{r} 33 \\ \times\ 3 \\ \hline \end{array}$$
$$\begin{array}{r} 32 \\ \times\ 3 \\ \hline \end{array}$$
$$\begin{array}{r} 31 \\ \times\ 3 \\ \hline \end{array}$$
$$\begin{array}{r} 31 \\ \times\ 2 \\ \hline \end{array}$$
$$\begin{array}{r} 55 \\ \times\ 1 \\ \hline \end{array}$$

Multiplication with Some Regrouping

Solve each problem below.

1.
$$\begin{array}{r} {}^{1}15 \\ \times\ 3 \\ \hline \mathbf{45} \end{array}$$
$$\begin{array}{r} 10 \\ \times\ 6 \\ \hline \end{array}$$
$$\begin{array}{r} 12 \\ \times\ 4 \\ \hline \end{array}$$
$$\begin{array}{r} 13 \\ \times\ 6 \\ \hline \end{array}$$

2.
$$\begin{array}{r} 11 \\ \times\ 5 \\ \hline \end{array}$$
$$\begin{array}{r} 14 \\ \times\ 7 \\ \hline \end{array}$$
$$\begin{array}{r} 16 \\ \times\ 4 \\ \hline \end{array}$$
$$\begin{array}{r} 18 \\ \times\ 4 \\ \hline \end{array}$$

3.
$$\begin{array}{r} 25 \\ \times\ 3 \\ \hline \end{array}$$
$$\begin{array}{r} 27 \\ \times\ 5 \\ \hline \end{array}$$
$$\begin{array}{r} 21 \\ \times\ 9 \\ \hline \end{array}$$
$$\begin{array}{r} 23 \\ \times\ 8 \\ \hline \end{array}$$

4.
$$\begin{array}{r} 28 \\ \times\ 4 \\ \hline \end{array}$$
$$\begin{array}{r} 20 \\ \times\ 5 \\ \hline \end{array}$$
$$\begin{array}{r} 29 \\ \times\ 3 \\ \hline \end{array}$$
$$\begin{array}{r} 26 \\ \times\ 6 \\ \hline \end{array}$$

5.
$$\begin{array}{r} 34 \\ \times\ 4 \\ \hline \end{array}$$
$$\begin{array}{r} 36 \\ \times\ 3 \\ \hline \end{array}$$
$$\begin{array}{r} 39 \\ \times\ 5 \\ \hline \end{array}$$
$$\begin{array}{r} 33 \\ \times\ 4 \\ \hline \end{array}$$

www.summerbridgeactivities.com © RBP Books

Multiplication with Some Regrouping

Solve each problem below.

1. $4 \times 8 =$ __**32**__ $9 \times 6 =$ _____

 $7 \times 9 =$ _____ $6 \times 5 =$ _____

2. $9 \times 8 =$ _____ $5 \times 7 =$ _____

 $3 \times 5 =$ _____ $4 \times 11 =$ _____

3. $12 \times 2 =$ _____ $7 \times 6 =$ _____

 $9 \times 9 =$ _____ $3 \times 12 =$ _____

4. $11 \times 7 =$ _____ $10 \times 3 =$ _____

 $6 \times 8 =$ _____ $8 \times 8 =$ _____

5. $5 \times 3 \times 2 =$ _____ $2 \times 6 \times 1 =$ _____

 $4 \times 10 \times 1 =$ _____ $7 \times 4 \times 8 =$ _____

6. $7 \times 2 \times 2 =$ _____ $4 \times 5 \times 2 =$ _____

 $3 \times 1 \times 6 =$ _____ $2 \times 8 \times 6 =$ _____

Multiplication with Some Regrouping

Solve each problem below.

7. 6 x 2 x 3 = _____   3 x 5 x 2 = _____

    4 x 3 x 3 = _____   8 x 4 x 2 = _____

8. 10 x 2 x 3 = _____   3 x 2 x 10 = _____

    5 x 2 x 10 = _____   0 x 5 x 8 = _____

9. 4 x 2 x 10 = _____   6 x 0 x 3 = _____

    12 x 3 x 0 = _____   1 x 9 x 2 = _____

10. 0 x 6 x 9 = _____   2 x 5 x 3 = _____

    0 x 7 x 8 = _____   10 x 5 x 1 = _____

11. 2 x 3 x 5 = _____   4 x 2 x 4 = _____

    7 x 3 x 2 = _____   12 x 2 x 1 = _____

12. 9 x 1 x 4 = _____   3 x 4 x 3 = _____

    2 x 9 x 3 = _____   6 x 1 x 11 = _____

2-Digit Multiplication with Some Regrouping

Solve each problem below.

1.
$$\begin{array}{r}54\\ \times\ 2\\ \hline \mathbf{108}\end{array}$$
$$\begin{array}{r}90\\ \times\ 2\\ \hline\end{array}$$
$$\begin{array}{r}47\\ \times\ 2\\ \hline\end{array}$$
$$\begin{array}{r}35\\ \times\ 2\\ \hline\end{array}$$
$$\begin{array}{r}62\\ \times\ 2\\ \hline\end{array}$$

2.
$$\begin{array}{r}17\\ \times\ 3\\ \hline\end{array}$$
$$\begin{array}{r}72\\ \times\ 3\\ \hline\end{array}$$
$$\begin{array}{r}23\\ \times\ 3\\ \hline\end{array}$$
$$\begin{array}{r}46\\ \times\ 3\\ \hline\end{array}$$
$$\begin{array}{r}37\\ \times\ 3\\ \hline\end{array}$$

3.
$$\begin{array}{r}57\\ \times\ 4\\ \hline\end{array}$$
$$\begin{array}{r}54\\ \times\ 4\\ \hline\end{array}$$
$$\begin{array}{r}72\\ \times\ 4\\ \hline\end{array}$$
$$\begin{array}{r}95\\ \times\ 4\\ \hline\end{array}$$
$$\begin{array}{r}42\\ \times\ 4\\ \hline\end{array}$$

4.
$$\begin{array}{r}48\\ \times\ 5\\ \hline\end{array}$$
$$\begin{array}{r}33\\ \times\ 5\\ \hline\end{array}$$
$$\begin{array}{r}90\\ \times\ 5\\ \hline\end{array}$$
$$\begin{array}{r}72\\ \times\ 5\\ \hline\end{array}$$
$$\begin{array}{r}86\\ \times\ 5\\ \hline\end{array}$$

5.
$$\begin{array}{r}37\\ \times\ 6\\ \hline\end{array}$$
$$\begin{array}{r}58\\ \times\ 6\\ \hline\end{array}$$
$$\begin{array}{r}40\\ \times\ 6\\ \hline\end{array}$$
$$\begin{array}{r}10\\ \times\ 6\\ \hline\end{array}$$
$$\begin{array}{r}65\\ \times\ 6\\ \hline\end{array}$$

2-Digit Multiplication with Some Regrouping

Solve each problem below.

1.
$$
\begin{array}{r} \overset{4}{1}7 \\ \times\ 7 \\ \hline \mathbf{119} \end{array}
\qquad
\begin{array}{r} 19 \\ \times\ 7 \\ \hline \end{array}
\qquad
\begin{array}{r} 23 \\ \times\ 7 \\ \hline \end{array}
\qquad
\begin{array}{r} 46 \\ \times\ 7 \\ \hline \end{array}
\qquad
\begin{array}{r} 37 \\ \times\ 7 \\ \hline \end{array}
$$

2.
$$
\begin{array}{r} 63 \\ \times\ 8 \\ \hline \end{array}
\qquad
\begin{array}{r} 21 \\ \times\ 8 \\ \hline \end{array}
\qquad
\begin{array}{r} 92 \\ \times\ 8 \\ \hline \end{array}
\qquad
\begin{array}{r} 83 \\ \times\ 8 \\ \hline \end{array}
\qquad
\begin{array}{r} 47 \\ \times\ 8 \\ \hline \end{array}
$$

3.
$$
\begin{array}{r} 84 \\ \times\ 9 \\ \hline \end{array}
\qquad
\begin{array}{r} 27 \\ \times\ 9 \\ \hline \end{array}
\qquad
\begin{array}{r} 90 \\ \times\ 9 \\ \hline \end{array}
\qquad
\begin{array}{r} 57 \\ \times\ 9 \\ \hline \end{array}
\qquad
\begin{array}{r} 75 \\ \times\ 9 \\ \hline \end{array}
$$

4.
$$
\begin{array}{r} 72 \\ \times\ 10 \\ \hline \end{array}
\qquad
\begin{array}{r} 97 \\ \times\ 10 \\ \hline \end{array}
\qquad
\begin{array}{r} 36 \\ \times\ 10 \\ \hline \end{array}
\qquad
\begin{array}{r} 44 \\ \times\ 10 \\ \hline \end{array}
\qquad
\begin{array}{r} 85 \\ \times\ 10 \\ \hline \end{array}
$$

5.
$$
\begin{array}{r} 54 \\ \times\ 2 \\ \hline \end{array}
\qquad
\begin{array}{r} 39 \\ \times\ 4 \\ \hline \end{array}
\qquad
\begin{array}{r} 65 \\ \times\ 6 \\ \hline \end{array}
\qquad
\begin{array}{r} 76 \\ \times\ 8 \\ \hline \end{array}
\qquad
\begin{array}{r} 59 \\ \times\ 10 \\ \hline \end{array}
$$

www.summerbridgeactivities.com

2-Digit Multiplication with Some Regrouping

Solve each problem below.

1. $\overset{2}{6}3$ 65   69   64   67
    x 7   x 3   x 5   x 9   x 7
    441

2. 77   71   70   75   76
    x 5   x 9   x 6   x 8   x 4

3. 82   85   89   83   88
    x 7   x 6   x 3   x 9   x 5

4. 90   92   96   95   99
    x 7   x 9   x 8   x 6   x 4

5. 62   79   86   94   39
    x 8   x 7   x 7   x 5   x 8

2-Digit Multiplication with Some Regrouping

Solve each problem below.

1.
$$\overset{4}{3}7 \times 6 = \mathbf{222}$$

35	36	38
x 2	x 8	x 7

2.

40	45	46	48
x 6	x 3	x 7	x 5

3.

42	44	47	49
x 9	x 8	x 7	x 4

4.

52	57	55	59
x 7	x 4	x 8	x 3

5.

53	58	57	56
x 9	x 6	x 5	x 7

Word Problem Solving

Read and solve the problems. Show your work in the box.
Write your answer on the line.

1.

Jimmy wanted to bring cookies to share with his class. He wanted each student to get 3 cookies. He has 29 students in his class.

How many cookies does he need to bring?

$$\begin{array}{r} ^{2}29 \\ \times\ 3 \\ \hline \mathbf{87} \end{array}$$

__87 cookies__

2.

Kara had 7 feet of ribbon.

She knows there are 12 inches in each foot.

How many inches of ribbon does she have?

_____

3.

Tina rode her bike 17 miles each day for 6 days.

How many miles did Tina ride?

_____

4.

Jack read 7 books.

Each book had 48 pages.

How many pages did Jack read?

_____

5.

Marissa has 5 trading card books.

Each book has 50 cards in it.

How many trading cards does Marissa have?

_____

I'm sure you'll have no problem finishing these problems!

Multiplication by Tens

Solve the problems.
Look for a pattern.

1.
24	33	77	9	3
x 10	x 10	x 10	x 10	x 10
240				

2.
4	44	7	42	72
x 10	x 10	x 10	x 10	x 10

3.
28	86	51	29	82
x 10	x 10	x 10	x 10	x 10

4.
8	23	66	83	13
x 10	x 10	x 10	x 10	x 10

5.
17	35	42	18	99
x 10	x 10	x 10	x 10	x 10

Complete each equation.

Multiplication Grade 3—RBP3764

3-Digit Multiplication with Some Regrouping

Solve each problem below.

1.
$$311 \times 8 = 2{,}488$$

$$248 \times 2$$

$$225 \times 4$$

$$283 \times 3$$

2.
$$143 \times 7$$

$$215 \times 3$$

$$103 \times 8$$

$$150 \times 5$$

3.
$$999 \times 2$$

$$274 \times 2$$

$$103 \times 9$$

$$208 \times 4$$

4.
$$401 \times 9$$

$$210 \times 4$$

$$252 \times 3$$

$$200 \times 6$$

5.
$$111 \times 8$$

$$521 \times 7$$

$$411 \times 9$$

$$517 \times 6$$

3-Digit Multiplication with Some Regrouping

6.

108	162	136	510
x 8	x 4	x 3	x 7

7.

907	485	271	704
x 7	x 2	x 9	x 8

8.

112	235	362	125
x 6	x 5	x 3	x 8

9.

422	891	107	790
x 4	x 6	x 9	x 5

10.

402	121	345	930
x 4	x 7	x 6	x 2

Multiplication with Money and Some Regrouping

Solve each problem below.

1.
$\quad$ $\overset{1}{\$1.03}$ $\qquad$ $\$2.10$ $\qquad$ $\$3.20$ $\qquad$ $\$2.32$
$\quad$ $\underline{\times\ \ \ \ 4}$ $\qquad$ $\underline{\times\ \ \ \ 3}$ $\qquad$ $\underline{\times\ \ \ \ 3}$ $\qquad$ $\underline{\times\ \ \ \ 2}$
$\quad$ **$4.12**

2.
$\quad$ $\$1.06$ $\qquad$ $\$3.11$ $\qquad$ $\$\ .60$ $\qquad$ $\$3.52$
$\quad$ $\underline{\times\ \ \ \ 4}$ $\qquad$ $\underline{\times\ \ \ \ 3}$ $\qquad$ $\underline{\times\ \ \ \ 5}$ $\qquad$ $\underline{\times\ \ \ \ 3}$

3.
$\quad$ $\$6.90$ $\qquad$ $\$\ .85$ $\qquad$ $\$1.33$ $\qquad$ $\$2.63$
$\quad$ $\underline{\times\ \ \ \ 2}$ $\qquad$ $\underline{\times\ \ \ \ 7}$ $\qquad$ $\underline{\times\ \ \ \ 4}$ $\qquad$ $\underline{\times\ \ \ \ 3}$

4.
$\quad$ $\$3.90$ $\qquad$ $\$1.78$ $\qquad$ $\$2.80$ $\qquad$ $\$5.05$
$\quad$ $\underline{\times\ \ \ \ 3}$ $\qquad$ $\underline{\times\ \ \ \ 5}$ $\qquad$ $\underline{\times\ \ \ \ 6}$ $\qquad$ $\underline{\times\ \ \ \ 4}$

5.
$\quad$ $\$6.07$ $\qquad$ $\$2.12$ $\qquad$ $\$3.90$ $\qquad$ $\$1.78$
$\quad$ $\underline{\times\ \ \ \ 2}$ $\qquad$ $\underline{\times\ \ \ \ 7}$ $\qquad$ $\underline{\times\ \ \ \ 9}$ $\qquad$ $\underline{\times\ \ \ \ 5}$

6. $2.80 $5.05 $6.07 $2.12
　　x　7   x　6   x　8   x　9

7. $4.22 $9.30 $3.64 $3.45
　　x　4   x　2   x　3   x　6

8. $8.07 $5.17 $5.00 $5.41
　　x　7   x　6   x　8   x　8

9. $3.14 $6.15 $7.33 $9.19
　　x　7   x　6   x　7   x　3

10. $3.87 $4.77 $6.92 $5.56
　　x　4   x　6   x　5   x　8

39

Estimation

Estimate first, then multiply to find the answer.

1.

$$\overset{2}{3}5 \times 5 \qquad 18 \times 6 \qquad 41 \times 7$$

Estimate $\underline{\mathbf{155}}$ _____ _____

Multiply $\underline{\mathbf{175}}$ _____ _____

> By my estimation these problems should be easy for a brain like you!

2.

$$24 \times 8 \qquad 25 \times 9 \qquad 63 \times 5 \qquad 94 \times 6$$

Estimate _____ _____ _____ _____

Multiply _____ _____ _____ _____

3.

$$112 \times 6 \qquad 107 \times 9 \qquad 206 \times 5 \qquad 410 \times 8$$

Estimate _____ _____ _____ _____

Multiply _____ _____ _____ _____

www.summerbridgeactivities.com

4.

	525	329	416	620
	x 3	x 4	x 7	x 5
Estimate	_____	_____	_____	_____
Multiply	_____	_____	_____	_____

5.

	314	910	490	377
	x 7	x 6	x 8	x 5
Estimate	_____	_____	_____	_____
Multiply	_____	_____	_____	_____

6.

	37	325	712	275
	x 4	x 7	x 2	x 9
Estimate	_____	_____	_____	_____
Multiply	_____	_____	_____	_____

Multiplication Grade 3—RBP3764

Word Problem Solving

Read and solve the problems. Show your work in the box.
Write your answer on the line.

1.

Randy had 6 bags.

He put 12 marbles in each bag.

How many marbles did he have?

$$
\begin{array}{r}
{}^{1}1\,2 \\
\times\ 6 \\
\hline
72
\end{array}
$$

__**72 marbles**__

2.

Jack read 7 books.

Each book had 64 pages.

How many pages did Jack read?

3.

Zach plays basketball 3 times each week. There are 52 weeks in a year.

How many times does he play in one year?

4.

The skaters skated in 7 groups with 14 in each group.

How many skaters were present in all of the groups?

5.

Juan put his penny collection into 4 bottles.

He put 234 pennies in each bottle.

How many pennies does he have in all?

I ♡ word problems!

2-Digit Multiplication with Some Regrouping

Solve each problem.

1.

^{4}
16   13   18   14   15

x 7   x 2   x 6   x 5   x 12

112

2.
18   14   16   17   14

x 1   x 9   x 3   x 8   x 10

3.
15   13   18   15   18

x 13   x 6   x 7   x 9   x 12

4.
13   17   15   14   18

x 10 x 13   x 4   x 12   x 4

5.
17   15   14   17   12

x 11 x 15   x 6   x 2   x 4

2-Digit Multiplication with Some Regrouping

Solve each problem below.

1.
    13   17   16   12
  x 5   x 8   x 4   x 3
  65

2.
    15   18   19   10
  x 9   x 1   x 6   x 7

3.
    24   28   26   21
  x 5   x 8   x 2   x 0

4.
    20   22   27   25
  x 9   x 7   x 4   x 2

5.
    36   38   30   31
  x 6   x 8   x 7   x 1

Number Puzzle

Complete the puzzle below. Spell out your number answer.

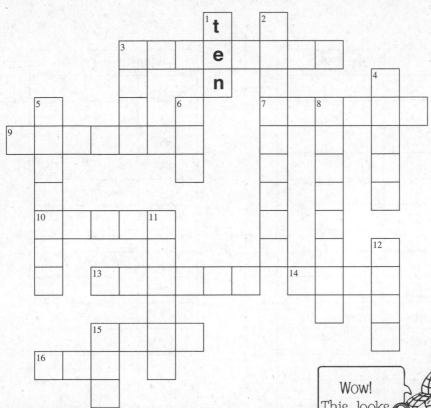

Wow! This looks like quite a puzzle!

Across

3. 1 x 19 =

7. 11 x 1 =

9. 4 x 4 =

10. 4 x 2 =

13. 10 x 2 =

14. 12 x 0 =

15. 5 x 1 =

16. 2 x 1 =

Down

1. 5 x 2 = **ten**

2. 17 x 1 =

3. 3 x 3 =

4. 1 x 7 =

5. 3 x 5 =

6. 1 x 1 =

8. 9 x 2 =

11. 3 x 4 =

12. 4 x 1 =

15. 2 x 2 =

Multiplication with Some Regrouping

Solve each problem below.

1.

Multiply by 5	
10	**50**
20	
30	
40	
50	
60	

2.

Multiply by 4	
5	
15	
25	
35	
45	
55	

3.

Multiply by 2	
23	
33	
43	
53	
63	
73	

4.

Multiply by 7	
27	
37	
47	
57	
67	
77	

5.

Multiply by 6	
22	
32	
42	
52	
62	
72	

6.

Multiply by 3	
24	
34	
44	
54	
64	
74	

Tables with Some Regrouping: 0–20

Solve each problem.

1.

2 x 4 = _____

4 x 4 = _____

6 x 4 = _____

8 x 4 = _____

10 x 4 = _____

12 x 4 = _____

14 x 4 = _____

16 x 4 = _____

18 x 4 = _____

20 x 4 = _____

2.

2 x 5 = _____

5 x 5 = _____

6 x 5 = _____

8 x 5 = _____

10 x 5 = _____

12 x 5 = _____

15 x 5 = _____

16 x 5 = _____

18 x 5 = _____

20 x 5 = _____

3.

2 x 6 = _____

6 x 6 = _____

7 x 6 = _____

8 x 6 = _____

10 x 6 = _____

12 x 6 = _____

16 x 6 = _____

17 x 6 = _____

18 x 6 = _____

20 x 6 = _____

4.

2 x 7 = _____

7 x 7 = _____

6 x 7 = _____

8 x 7 = _____

10 x 7 = _____

12 x 7 = _____

17 x 7 = _____

16 x 7 = _____

18 x 7 = _____

20 x 7 = _____

Solve each problem below.

1.

$$\begin{array}{r} {\scriptstyle 1\ 2} \\ 425 \\ \times\ 4 \\ \hline \mathbf{1{,}700} \end{array}$$

$$\begin{array}{r} 693 \\ \times\ 3 \\ \hline \end{array}$$

$$\begin{array}{r} 748 \\ \times\ 9 \\ \hline \end{array}$$

$$\begin{array}{r} 681 \\ \times\ 2 \\ \hline \end{array}$$

2.

$$\begin{array}{r} 523 \\ \times\ 8 \\ \hline \end{array}$$

$$\begin{array}{r} 398 \\ \times\ 1 \\ \hline \end{array}$$

$$\begin{array}{r} 544 \\ \times\ 5 \\ \hline \end{array}$$

$$\begin{array}{r} 210 \\ \times\ 7 \\ \hline \end{array}$$

3.

$$\begin{array}{r} 112 \\ \times\ 6 \\ \hline \end{array}$$

$$\begin{array}{r} 999 \\ \times\ 4 \\ \hline \end{array}$$

$$\begin{array}{r} 823 \\ \times\ 8 \\ \hline \end{array}$$

$$\begin{array}{r} 498 \\ \times\ 3 \\ \hline \end{array}$$

4.

$$\begin{array}{r} 511 \\ \times\ 2 \\ \hline \end{array}$$

$$\begin{array}{r} 225 \\ \times\ 9 \\ \hline \end{array}$$

$$\begin{array}{r} 176 \\ \times\ 4 \\ \hline \end{array}$$

$$\begin{array}{r} 621 \\ \times\ 5 \\ \hline \end{array}$$

5.

$$\begin{array}{r} 844 \\ \times\ 7 \\ \hline \end{array}$$

$$\begin{array}{r} 929 \\ \times\ 3 \\ \hline \end{array}$$

$$\begin{array}{r} 279 \\ \times\ 6 \\ \hline \end{array}$$

$$\begin{array}{r} 681 \\ \times\ 2 \\ \hline \end{array}$$

3-Digit Multiplication with Some Regrouping

Good job! You didn't even have to take off your shoes!

6.	498 x 5	161 x 3	743 x 4	628 x 9
7.	912 x 2	283 x 7	470 x 5	682 x 6
8.	180 x 8	367 x 4	525 x 3	945 x 5
9.	308 x 9	744 x 4	618 x 2	428 x 6
10.	505 x 7	699 x 3	422 x 5	820 x 8

49

Growing and Mowing

Solve each problem.

1. Max needs 48 pounds of grass seed for each lawn he plants. If Max plants 3 lawns, how many pounds of grass seed will he need?

$$\begin{array}{r} 2 \\ 48 \\ \underline{\times\ 3} \\ \mathbf{144} \end{array}$$ **pounds of grass seed**

2. Spencer is planting tomato plants. There are 5 rows of 47 tomato plants. How many tomato plants did Spencer plant altogether?

3. Lizzie has 17 watering cans. Each watering can holds 6 gallons of water. How many gallons of water will it take to fill all 17 watering cans?

4. Jess is putting fertilizer on 23 lawns. He needs 4 bags of fertilizer for each lawn. How many bags of fertilizer will Jess need to buy?

5. Sara is mowing lawns for the summer. She mows 5 lawns a week. If Sara mows lawns for 23 weeks, how many lawns will she mow altogether?

6. Kyle has 3 times as many garden tools as Anne. Anne has 37 garden tools. How many garden tools does Kyle have?

7. Josh plants 59 squash plants. Each plant has 6 squash growing on the vine. How many squash does Josh have?

Emmett is helping his brother in the pet store after school. Help him find the answer to each problem.

1. Emmett is going to feed the rabbits. There are 11 cages with 4 rabbits in each cage. How many rabbits will Emmett need to feed?

    $$\begin{array}{r} 11 \\ \times\,4 \\ \hline \textbf{44} \ \textbf{rabbits} \end{array}$$

2. The pet store sells 2 times as many red pet collars as blue pet collars. Emmett sells 42 blue pet collars. How many red pet collars does Emmett sell?

3. There are 21 turtles. Emmett feeds 2 lettuce leaves to each turtle. How many lettuce leaves does it take to feed the turtles?

4. Emmett helps take the dogs for a walk. There are 3 times as many poodles as cocker spaniels. There are 13 cocker spaniels. How many poodles are there?

5. Emmett is ordering more canary seed for the pet store. If the canaries eat 4 bags of seed in a month, how many bags will Emmett need to order for the next 12 months?

6. The iguanas eat 3 times a week. How many times will Emmett need to feed the iguanas in the next 32 weeks?

7. Emmett sells 3 times as many dog toys as cat toys. Emmett sells 23 cat toys. How many dog toys does Emmett sell?

Multiplication Puzzle

Start from the center and work outward to answer each problem.

Check yourself with a calculator!

© RBP Books

Bookworm Bonanza

Solve each problem.

1. Hillary reads 842 pages a week. How many pages will Hillary read in 9 weeks?

   $$\begin{array}{r} \scriptstyle 3\,1 \\ 842 \\ \times\quad 9 \\ \hline 7{,}578 \end{array}$$ **pages**

2. Each day, 328 people come to the library. How many people will come to the library in a week?

3. Each magazine box holds 9 magazines. The library has 528 full magazine boxes. How many magazines does the library have?

4. Gary checked out 467 books in a year. Kristen checked out 3 times as many books as Gary. How many books did Kristen check out?

5. The Southtown Library has 8 times as many books as the Littleton Library. The Littleton Library has 356 books. How many books does the Southtown Library have?

Extra! Extra!

Solve each problem.

1. Jonathan delivers 9 newspapers. He gets paid $1.14 for each newspaper he delivers. How much money does Jonathan earn?

$$\begin{array}{r} \$1.14 \\ \underline{\times\ 9} \\ \$10.26 \end{array}$$

2. Annie places an ad in the newspaper. The newspaper charges 5¢ a word. Annie's ad has 694 words. How much does the ad cost Annie?

3. Desi spends twice as much at the newsstand as Meg. Meg spends $58.31. How much does Desi spend?

4. The *Daily Times* sells 3,491 newspapers for 4¢ each. How much money does the *Daily Times* make?

5. Tara buys 3 newspapers that cost $3.95 each. She gives the clerk $20.00. How much change does Tara get back?

6. Belle gets paid 9¢ for each word she writes. Belle writes 4,593 words. How much money does Belle earn?

Party Planning

Solve each problem.

1. Samantha buys 63 boxes of cupcakes for her birthday party. Each box has 4 cupcakes. How many cupcakes does she have?

   63
   x 4
   252 cupcakes

2. Jill buys 349 party favors for 7¢ each. How much does Jill spend?

3. Bill has 14 6-packs of soda. How many cans of soda does he have?

4. A bunch of 12 balloons costs $13.99. If Marissa buys 3 bunches, how much does she spend on balloons?

5. Vivian has 66 packages of party hats. Each package contains 6 party hats. How many party hats does Vivian have?

6. Amanda puts up decorations. She has 32 7-inch pieces of ribbon. How many inches of ribbon does she have in all?

55

Fill in the charts to complete the times tables. Record your best time.

Forward	Backwards	Free-for-All
Time _____	Time _____	Time _____
2 x 0 = ___	2 x 12 = ___	2 x 7 = ___
2 x 1 = ___	2 x 11 = ___	2 x 5 = ___
2 x 2 = ___	2 x 10 = ___	2 x 1 = ___
2 x 3 = ___	2 x 9 = ___	2 x 12 = ___
2 x 4 = ___	2 x 8 = ___	2 x 9 = ___
2 x 5 = ___	2 x 7 = ___	2 x 2 = ___
2 x 6 = ___	2 x 6 = ___	2 x 4 = ___
2 x 7 = ___	2 x 5 = ___	2 x 11 = ___
2 x 8 = ___	2 x 4 = ___	2 x 6 = ___
2 x 9 = ___	2 x 3 = ___	2 x 8 = ___
2 x 10 = ___	2 x 2 = ___	2 x 0 = ___
2 x 11 = ___	2 x 1 = ___	2 x 3 = ___
2 x 12 = ___	2 x 0 = ___	2 x 10 = ___

Fill in the charts to complete the times tables. Record your best time.

Forward	Backwards	Free-for-All
Time _____	Time _____	Time _____
3 x 0 = ___	3 x 12 = ___	3 x 7 = ___
3 x 1 = ___	3 x 11 = ___	3 x 5 = ___
3 x 2 = ___	3 x 10 = ___	3 x 1 = ___
3 x 3 = ___	3 x 9 = ___	3 x 12 = ___
3 x 4 = ___	3 x 8 = ___	3 x 9 = ___
3 x 5 = ___	3 x 7 = ___	3 x 2 = ___
3 x 6 = ___	3 x 6 = ___	3 x 4 = ___
3 x 7 = ___	3 x 5 = ___	3 x 11 = ___
3 x 8 = ___	3 x 4 = ___	3 x 6 = ___
3 x 9 = ___	3 x 3 = ___	3 x 8 = ___
3 x 10 = ___	3 x 2 = ___	3 x 0 = ___
3 x 11 = ___	3 x 1 = ___	3 x 3 = ___
3 x 12 = ___	3 x 0 = ___	3 x 10 = ___

Times Tables: 4

Fill in the charts to complete the times tables. Record your best time.

Forward	Backwards	Free-for-All
Time ____	Time ____	Time ____
4 x 0 = ___	4 x 12 = ___	4 x 7 = ___
4 x 1 = ___	4 x 11 = ___	4 x 5 = ___
4 x 2 = ___	4 x 10 = ___	4 x 1 = ___
4 x 3 = ___	4 x 9 = ___	4 x 12 = ___
4 x 4 = ___	4 x 8 = ___	4 x 9 = ___
4 x 5 = ___	4 x 7 = ___	4 x 2 = ___
4 x 6 = ___	4 x 6 = ___	4 x 4 = ___
4 x 7 = ___	4 x 5 = ___	4 x 11 = ___
4 x 8 = ___	4 x 4 = ___	4 x 6 = ___
4 x 9 = ___	4 x 3 = ___	4 x 8 = ___
4 x 10 = ___	4 x 2 = ___	4 x 0 = ___
4 x 11 = ___	4 x 1 = ___	4 x 3 = ___
4 x 12 = ___	4 x 0 = ___	4 x 10 = ___

Fill in the charts to complete the times tables. Record your best time.

Forward	Backwards	Free-for-All
Time _____	Time _____	Time _____
5 x 0 = ___	5 x 12 = ___	5 x 7 = ___
5 x 1 = ___	5 x 11 = ___	5 x 5 = ___
5 x 2 = ___	5 x 10 = ___	5 x 1 = ___
5 x 3 = ___	5 x 9 = ___	5 x 12 = ___
5 x 4 = ___	5 x 8 = ___	5 x 9 = ___
5 x 5 = ___	5 x 7 = ___	5 x 2 = ___
5 x 6 = ___	5 x 6 = ___	5 x 4 = ___
5 x 7 = ___	5 x 5 = ___	5 x 11 = ___
5 x 8 = ___	5 x 4 = ___	5 x 6 = ___
5 x 9 = ___	5 x 3 = ___	5 x 8 = ___
5 x 10 = ___	5 x 2 = ___	5 x 0 = ___
5 x 11 = ___	5 x 1 = ___	5 x 3 = ___
5 x 12 = ___	5 x 0 = ___	5 x 10 = ___

Fill in the charts to complete the times tables. Record your best time.

Forward	Backwards	Free-for-All
Time _____	Time _____	Time _____
6 x 0 = ___	6 x 12 = ___	6 x 7 = ___
6 x 1 = ___	6 x 11 = ___	6 x 5 = ___
6 x 2 = ___	6 x 10 = ___	6 x 1 = ___
6 x 3 = ___	6 x 9 = ___	6 x 12 = ___
6 x 4 = ___	6 x 8 = ___	6 x 9 = ___
6 x 5 = ___	6 x 7 = ___	6 x 2 = ___
6 x 6 = ___	6 x 6 = ___	6 x 4 = ___
6 x 7 = ___	6 x 5 = ___	6 x 11 = ___
6 x 8 = ___	6 x 4 = ___	6 x 6 = ___
6 x 9 = ___	6 x 3 = ___	6 x 8 = ___
6 x 10 = ___	6 x 2 = ___	6 x 0 = ___
6 x 11 = ___	6 x 1 = ___	6 x 3 = ___
6 x 12 = ___	6 x 0 = ___	6 x 10 = ___

Fill in the charts to complete the times tables. Record your best time.

Forward	Backwards	Free-for-All
Time _____	Time _____	Time _____
7 x 0 = ___	7 x 12 = ___	7 x 7 = ___
7 x 1 = ___	7 x 11 = ___	7 x 5 = ___
7 x 2 = ___	7 x 10 = ___	7 x 1 = ___
7 x 3 = ___	7 x 9 = ___	7 x 12 = ___
7 x 4 = ___	7 x 8 = ___	7 x 9 = ___
7 x 5 = ___	7 x 7 = ___	7 x 2 = ___
7 x 6 = ___	7 x 6 = ___	7 x 4 = ___
7 x 7 = ___	7 x 5 = ___	7 x 11 = ___
7 x 8 = ___	7 x 4 = ___	7 x 6 = ___
7 x 9 = ___	7 x 3 = ___	7 x 8 = ___
7 x 10 = ___	7 x 2 = ___	7 x 0 = ___
7 x 11 = ___	7 x 1 = ___	7 x 3 = ___
7 x 12 = ___	7 x 0 = ___	7 x 10 = ___

Multiplication Grade 3—RBP3764

Fill in the charts to complete the times tables. Record your best time.

Forward	Backwards	Free-for-All
Time _____	Time _____	Time _____
8 x 0 = ___	8 x 12 = ___	8 x 7 = ___
8 x 1 = ___	8 x 11 = ___	8 x 5 = ___
8 x 2 = ___	8 x 10 = ___	8 x 1 = ___
8 x 3 = ___	8 x 9 = ___	8 x 12 = ___
8 x 4 = ___	8 x 8 = ___	8 x 9 = ___
8 x 5 = ___	8 x 7 = ___	8 x 2 = ___
8 x 6 = ___	8 x 6 = ___	8 x 4 = ___
8 x 7 = ___	8 x 5 = ___	8 x 11 = ___
8 x 8 = ___	8 x 4 = ___	8 x 6 = ___
8 x 9 = ___	8 x 3 = ___	8 x 8 = ___
8 x 10 = ___	8 x 2 = ___	8 x 0 = ___
8 x 11 = ___	8 x 1 = ___	8 x 3 = ___
8 x 12 = ___	8 x 0 = ___	8 x 10 = ___

Fill in the charts to complete the times tables. Record your best time.

Forward	Backwards	Free-for-All
Time _____	Time _____	Time _____
9 x 0 = ___	9 x 12 = ___	9 x 7 = ___
9 x 1 = ___	9 x 11 = ___	9 x 5 = ___
9 x 2 = ___	9 x 10 = ___	9 x 1 = ___
9 x 3 = ___	9 x 9 = ___	9 x 12 = ___
9 x 4 = ___	9 x 8 = ___	9 x 9 = ___
9 x 5 = ___	9 x 7 = ___	9 x 2 = ___
9 x 6 = ___	9 x 6 = ___	9 x 4 = ___
9 x 7 = ___	9 x 5 = ___	9 x 11 = ___
9 x 8 = ___	9 x 4 = ___	9 x 6 = ___
9 x 9 = ___	9 x 3 = ___	9 x 8 = ___
9 x 10 = ___	9 x 2 = ___	9 x 0 = ___
9 x 11 = ___	9 x 1 = ___	9 x 3 = ___
9 x 12 = ___	9 x 0 = ___	9 x 10 = ___

Fill in the charts to complete the times tables. Record your best time.

Forward	Backwards	Free-for-All
Time _____	Time _____	Time _____
10 x 0 = ___	10 x 12 = ___	10 x 7 = ___
10 x 1 = ___	10 x 11 = ___	10 x 5 = ___
10 x 2 = ___	10 x 10 = ___	10 x 1 = ___
10 x 3 = ___	10 x 9 = ___	10 x 12 = ___
10 x 4 = ___	10 x 8 = ___	10 x 9 = ___
10 x 5 = ___	10 x 7 = ___	10 x 2 = ___
10 x 6 = ___	10 x 6 = ___	10 x 4 = ___
10 x 7 = ___	10 x 5 = ___	10 x 11 = ___
10 x 8 = ___	10 x 4 = ___	10 x 6 = ___
10 x 9 = ___	10 x 3 = ___	10 x 8 = ___
10 x 10 = ___	10 x 2 = ___	10 x 0 = ___
10 x 11 = ___	10 x 1 = ___	10 x 3 = ___
10 x 12 = ___	10 x 0 = ___	10 x 10 = ___

Fill in the charts to complete the times tables. Record your best time.

Forward
Time _____

11 x 0 = ___

11 x 1 = ___

11 x 2 = ___

11 x 3 = ___

11 x 4 = ___

11 x 5 = ___

11 x 6 = ___

11 x 7 = ___

11 x 8 = ___

11 x 9 = ___

11 x 10 = ___

11 x 11 = ___

11 x 12 = ___

Backwards
Time _____

11 x 12 = ___

11 x 11 = ___

11 x 10 = ___

11 x 9 = ___

11 x 8 = ___

11 x 7 = ___

11 x 6 = ___

11 x 5 = ___

11 x 4 = ___

11 x 3 = ___

11 x 2 = ___

11 x 1 = ___

11 x 0 = ___

Free-for-All
Time _____

11 x 7 = ___

11 x 5 = ___

11 x 1 = ___

11 x 12 = ___

11 x 9 = ___

11 x 2 = ___

11 x 4 = ___

11 x 11 = ___

11 x 6 = ___

11 x 8 = ___

11 x 0 = ___

11 x 3 = ___

11 x 10 = ___

Multiplication Grade 3—RBP3764

Fill in the charts to complete the times tables. Record your best time.

Forward	Backwards	Free-for-All
Time _____	Time _____	Time _____
12 x 0 = ___	12 x 12 = ___	12 x 7 = ___
12 x 1 = ___	12 x 11 = ___	12 x 5 = ___
12 x 2 = ___	12 x 10 = ___	12 x 1 = ___
12 x 3 = ___	12 x 9 = ___	12 x 12 = ___
12 x 4 = ___	12 x 8 = ___	12 x 9 = ___
12 x 5 = ___	12 x 7 = ___	12 x 2 = ___
12 x 6 = ___	12 x 6 = ___	12 x 4 = ___
12 x 7 = ___	12 x 5 = ___	12 x 11 = ___
12 x 8 = ___	12 x 4 = ___	12 x 6 = ___
12 x 9 = ___	12 x 3 = ___	12 x 8 = ___
12 x 10 = ___	12 x 2 = ___	12 x 0 = ___
12 x 11 = ___	12 x 1 = ___	12 x 3 = ___
12 x 12 = ___	12 x 0 = ___	12 x 10 = ___

Face Puzzles — Part 1

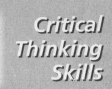

Ms. Hansen is creating mystery picture puzzles of Grayson, Lori and Tanner. Find out which pieces belong together by solving the equation below each puzzle piece.

Top:

693
x 3

748
x 9

681
x 2

Middle:

398
x 1

544
x 5

210
x 7

Bottom:

999
x 4

823
x 8

498
x 3

Face Puzzles — Part 2

Write the correct name below each set of answers.

Grayson

Lori

Tanner

1.

6732
398
1494

2.

2079
1470
6584

3.

1362
2720
3996

Pirate Treasure

The dread Pirate Marvin hid his treasure on Barracuda Island, but he left a trail of cargo along the way. Solve the first equation. The answer is the first number in the next equation. Draw a line from one equation to the next to sail your boat through the cargo trail to the treasure.

Start Here

2 x 2 =

7 x 7 =

4 x 5 =

24 x 2 =

140 x 3 =

20 x 7 =

420 x 6 =

2520

320 x 2 =

© RBP Books

Multiplication Grade 3—RBP3764

Secret Message

Denise left a coded message for Matt.
See if you can decode the note using the key.

Key:	A=1	B=2	C=3	D=4	E=5	F=6
	G=7	H=8	I=9	J=10	K=11	L=12
	M=13	N=14	O=15	P=16	Q=17	R=18
	S=19	T=20	U=21	V=22	W=23	X=24
	Y=25	Z=26				

$$\begin{array}{r} 1 \\ \times\ 3 \\ \hline \end{array} \qquad \begin{array}{r} 5 \\ \times\ 3 \\ \hline \end{array} \qquad \begin{array}{r} 13 \\ \times\ 1 \\ \hline \end{array} \qquad \begin{array}{r} 1 \\ \times\ 5 \\ \hline \end{array}$$

$$\begin{array}{r} 4 \\ \times\ 5 \\ \hline \end{array} \qquad \begin{array}{r} 3 \\ \times\ 5 \\ \hline \end{array} \qquad \begin{array}{r} 1 \\ \times\ 13 \\ \hline \end{array} \qquad \begin{array}{r} 5 \\ \times\ 5 \\ \hline \end{array}$$

I know you can solve this puzzle!

$$\begin{array}{r} 2 \\ \times\ 4 \\ \hline \end{array} \quad \begin{array}{r} 1 \\ \times 15 \\ \hline \end{array} \quad \begin{array}{r} 3 \\ \times\ 7 \\ \hline \end{array} \quad \begin{array}{r} 19 \\ \times\ 1 \\ \hline \end{array} \quad \begin{array}{r} 1 \\ \times\ 5 \\ \hline \end{array}$$

$$\begin{array}{r} 10 \\ \times\ 2 \\ \hline \end{array} \quad \begin{array}{r} 5 \\ \times\ 3 \\ \hline \end{array} \quad \begin{array}{r} 2 \\ \times\ 2 \\ \hline \end{array} \quad \begin{array}{r} 1 \\ \times\ 1 \\ \hline \end{array} \quad \begin{array}{r} 5 \\ \times\ 5 \\ \hline \end{array}$$

Larry the Lizard — Part 1

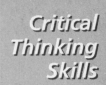

Grayson is pet-sitting his neighbor's lizard, Larry, while she is on vacation. How many times will Grayson need to feed Larry if his neighbor gets back on Tuesday April 2nd?

———————————————————————————

Tuesday, March 12

Dear Grayson,

Thank you so much for watching Larry while I am on my vacation. Please feed him 3 times a week. He also likes his tummy scratched. Thanks again!

Ms. Dean

Larry the Lizard — Part 2

March

S	M	T	W	T	F	S
					1	2
3	4	5	6	7	8	9
10	11	12	13	14	15	16
17	18	19	20	21	22	23
24/31	25	26	27	28	29	30

April

S	M	T	W	T	F	S
	1	2	3	4	5	6
7	8	9	10	11	12	13
14	15	16	17	18	19	20
21	22	23	24	25	26	27
28	29	30				

Bake Sale Cookies

Rob's mother left him a recipe to follow to make cookies for the bake sale. But there's one problem! His mother wrote the recipe using multiplication problems. Answer each equation; then write the corresponding ingredient on the line following it.

Mom's Marvelous
Multiplication Cookies

1/2 Cup **6 x 4**= _____ _____

2 Cups **9 x 5**= _____ _____

1 Cup **6 x 9**= _____ _____

2 **3 x 5**= _____ _____

1/4 Cup **7 x 6**= _____ _____

Mix together in a large bowl until well blended. Spoon onto a greased cookie sheet and bake for 12 minutes at 350°

Bananas
72

Chocolate Chips
9

Milk
24

Butter
42

Eggs
15

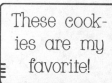

These cookies are my favorite!

Blueberries
12

Flour
45

Sugar
54

Alien Spaceship

The aliens on planet Grog had a huge party for the entire galaxy! They invited so many aliens that the guests can't find where they parked their spaceships. Help each alien find its spaceship by solving the equations on the ships and matching them to the alien with the correct answer on its tummy.

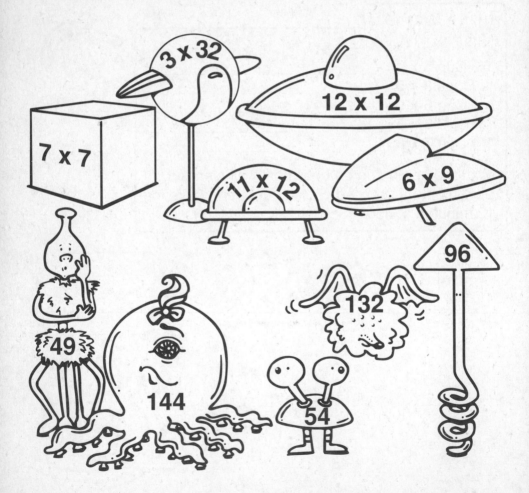

Answer Pages

Page 3

1. 2x4=8   4x2=8
2. 2x6=12   6x2=12
3. 3x4=12   4x3=12
4. 3x5=15   5x3=15
5. 2x5=10   5x2=10
6. 4x5=20   5x4=20

Page 4

1. 0, 0, 0, 0, 0, 0, 0, 0, 0, 0
2. 1, 2, 3, 4, 5, 6, 7, 8, 9
3. 2, 4, 6, 8, 10, 12, 14, 16, 18

Page 5

4. 3, 6, 9, 12, 15, 18, 21, 24, 27
5. 4, 8, 12, 16, 20, 24, 28, 32, 36
6. 5, 10, 15, 20, 25, 30, 35, 40, 45

Page 6

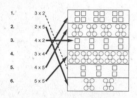

7. four groups of four
8. three groups of three
9. two groups of five
10. four groups of one

Page 7

1. 6, 12, 18, 24, 30, 36, 42, 48, 54
2. 7, 14, 21, 28, 35, 42, 49, 56, 63
3. 8, 16, 24, 32, 40, 48, 56, 64, 72
4. 9, 18, 27, 36, 45, 54, 63, 72, 81

Page 8

1. 8, 8   2. 15, 15   3. 6, 6
4. 10, 10   5. 21, 21   6. 12, 12
7. 18, 18   8. 24, 24   9. 14, 14
10. 6, 6   11. 16, 16   12. 36, 36

Page 9

x	1	2	3	4	5	6	7	8	9
1	1	2	3	4	5	6	7	8	9
2	2	4	6	8	10	12	14	16	18
3	3	6	9	12	15	18	21	24	27
4	4	8	12	16	20	24	28	32	36
5	5	10	15	20	25	30	35	40	45
6	6	12	18	24	30	36	42	48	54
7	7	14	21	28	35	42	49	56	63
8	8	16	24	32	40	48	56	64	72
9	9	18	27	36	45	54	63	72	81

1. Itself.
2. Count by 2s.
3. All end in 5 or 0.
4. They all add up to 9.
5. 12

Page 10

1. 4, 6, 15, 6, 12
2. 16, 10, 12, 8, 2
3. 14, 18, 18, 16, 20
4. 27, 30, 24, 21, 24
5. 16, 30, 40, 63, 64

Page 11

1. 54 marbles
2. 32 cards
3. 45 times
4. 30 miles
5. 28 skaters

Page 12

1. <   <
2. >   =
3. <   >
4. >   =
5. >   <
6. <   <
7. =   =
8. >   <

Answer Pages

Page 13
1. 18, 10, 6, 12, 14, 8, 4, 16
2. 45, 25, 15, 30, 35, 20, 10, 40
3. 27, 15, 9, 18, 21, 12, 6, 24
4. 54, 30, 18, 36, 42, 24, 12, 48
5. 81, 45, 27, 54, 63, 36, 18, 72
6. 36, 20, 12, 24, 28, 16, 8, 32

Page 14
1. 36, 35, 36; 56, 28, 15
2. 21, 54, 64; 40, 48, 45
3. 16, 42, 32; 27, 30, 32
4. 42, 72, 49; 35, 25, 48
5. 18, 48, 63; 54, 72, 21

Page 15
1. 30, 12, 32
2. 28, 40, 18
3. 36, 30, 36
4. 42, 54, 60
5. 16, 18, 0
6. 0, 0, 56

Page 16
1. 10, 20, 30, 40, 50, 60, 70, 80, 90
2. 11, 22, 33, 44, 55, 66, 77, 88, 99
3. 12, 24, 36, 48, 60, 72, 84, 96, 108

Page 17
1. 80, 30, 60, 20, 0
2. 50, 70, 40, 90, 10
3. 88, 33, 66, 22, 0
4. 55, 77, 44, 99, 11
5. 96, 36, 72, 24, 0

Page 18
6. 60 , 84, 48, 108, 12
7. 48, 22, 20, 30, 12
8. 33, 70, 36, 44, 10
9. 24, 60, 55, 60, 80
10. 90, 66, 50, 72, 77

Page 19
1. 7	2. 40	3. 9
4. 4	5. 4	6. 9
7. 12	8. 12	9. 24
10. 4	11. 6	12. 7

Page 20

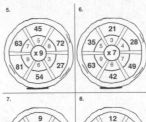

Page 21
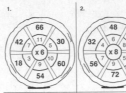

Page 22
1. 1, 7	2. 7, 8
3. 10 , 6	4. 9, 10
5. 6, 5	6. 20, 12
7. 0, 11	8. 7, 7
9. 4, 12	

Page 23
10. 0, 7	11. 10, 9
12. 10, 10	13. 9, 6
14. 12, 9	15. 9, 3
16. 8, 4	17. 11, 7
18. 9, 9	

Answer Pages

Page 24
1. 8x6=48   – 48 bandages
2. 3x8=24   – 24 tents
3. 4x9=36   – 36 tires
4. 3x12=36   – 36 feedings
5. 5x11=55   – 55 lawns

Page 25
1. 48, 22, 26, 39, 14
2. 33, 28, 36, 44, 69
3. 13, 66, 66, 64, 88
4. 84, 48, 44, 63, 77
5. 99, 96, 93, 62, 55

Page 26
1. 45, 60, 48, 78
2. 55, 98, 64, 72
3. 75, 135, 189, 184
4. 112, 100, 87, 156
5. 136, 108, 195, 132

Page 27
1. 32, 54;   63, 30
2. 72, 35;   15, 44
3. 24, 42;   81, 36
4. 77, 30;   48, 64
5. 30, 12;   40, 224
6. 28, 40;   18, 96

Page 28
7. 36, 30;   36, 63
8. 60, 60;   100, 0
9. 80, 0;   0, 18
10. 0, 30;   0, 50
11. 30, 32;   42, 24
12. 36, 36;   54, 66

Page 29
1. 108, 180, 94, 70, 124
2. 51, 216, 69, 138, 111
3. 228, 216, 288, 380, 168
4. 240, 165, 450, 360, 430
5. 222, 348, 240, 60, 390

Page 30
1. 119, 133, 161, 322, 259
2. 504, 168, 736, 664, 376
3. 756, 243, 810, 513, 675
4. 720, 970, 360, 440, 850
5. 108, 156, 390, 608, 590

Page 31
1. 441, 195, 345, 576, 469
2. 385, 639, 420, 600, 304
3. 574, 510, 267, 747, 440
4. 630, 828, 768, 570, 396
5. 496, 553, 602, 470, 312

Page 32
1. 222, 70, 288, 266
2. 240, 135, 322, 240
3. 378, 352, 329, 196
4. 364, 228, 440, 177
5. 477, 348, 285, 392

Page 33
1. 3x29=87   – 87 cookies
2. 7x12=84   – 84 inches of ribbon
3. 17x6=102   – 102 miles
4. 7x48=336   – 336 pages
5. 5x50=250   – 250 trading cards

Page 34
1. 240, 330, 770, 90, 30
2. 40, 440, 70, 420, 720
3. 280, 860, 510, 290, 820
4. 80, 230, 660, 830, 130
5. 170, 350, 420, 180, 990

Page 35

Answer Pages

Page 36
1. 2,488; 496; 900; 849
2. 1,001; 645; 824; 750
3. 1,998; 548; 927; 832
4. 3,609; 840; 756; 1,200
5. 888; 3,647; 3,699; 3,102

Page 37
6. 864; 648; 408; 3,570
7. 6,349; 970; 2,439; 5,632
8. 672; 1,175; 1,086; 1,000
9. 1,688; 5,346; 963; 3,950
10. 1,608; 847; 2,070; 1,860

Page 38
1. $4.12, $6.30, $9.60, $4.64
2. $4.24, $9.33, $3.00, $10.56
3. $13.80, $5.95, $5.32, $7.89
4. $11.70, $8.90, $16.80, $20.20
5. $12.14, $14.84, $35.10, $8.90

Page 39
6. $19.60, $30.30, $48.56, $19.08
7. $16.88, $18.60, $10.92, $20.70
8. $56.49, $31.02, $40.00, $43.28
9. $21.98, $36.90, $51.31, $27.57
10. $15.48, $28.62, $34.60, $44.48

Page 40
Estimates will vary.
1. 175, 108, 287
2. 192, 225, 315, 564
3. 672; 963; 1,030; 3,280

Page 41
Estimates will vary.
4. 1,575; 1,316; 2,912; 3,100
5. 2,198; 5,460; 3,920; 1,885
6. 148; 2,275; 1,424; 2,475

Page 42
1. 6x12=72   – 72 marbles
2. 7x64=448 – 448 pages read
3. 3x52=156 – 156 times a year
4. 7x14=98   – 98 skaters in all
5. 4x234=936– 936 pennies

Page 43
1. 112, 26, 108, 70, 180
2. 18, 126, 48, 136, 140
3. 195, 78, 126, 135, 216
4. 130, 221, 60, 168, 72
5. 187, 225, 84, 34, 48

Page 44
1. 65, 136, 64, 36
2. 135, 18, 114, 70
3. 120, 224, 52, 0
4. 180, 154, 108, 50
5. 216, 304, 210, 31

Page 45

Across	.Down
3. nineteen	1. ten
7. eleven	2. seventeen
9. sixteen	3. nine
10. eight	4. seven
13. twenty	5. fifteen
14. zero	6. one
15. five	8. eighteen
16. two	11. twelve
	12. four
	15. four

Page 46
1. 50, 100, 150, 200, 250, 300
2. 20, 60, 100, 140, 180, 220
3. 46, 66, 86, 106, 126, 146
4. 189, 259, 329, 399, 469, 539
5. 132, 192, 252, 312, 372, 432
6. 72, 102, 132, 162, 192, 222

Page 47
1. 8, 16, 24, 32, 40, 48, 56, 64, 72, 80
2. 10, 25, 30, 40, 50, 60, 75, 80, 90, 100
3. 12, 36, 42, 48, 60, 72, 96, 102, 108, 120
4. 14, 49, 42, 56, 70, 84, 119, 112, 126, 140

Answer Pages

Page 48
1. 1,700; 2,079; 6,732; 1,362
2. 4,184; 398; 2,720; 1,470
3. 672; 3,996; 6,584; 1,494
4. 1,022; 2,025; 704; 3,105
5. 5,908; 2,787; 1,674; 1,362

Page 49
6. 2,490; 483; 2,972; 5,652
7. 1,824; 1,981; 2,350, 4,092
8. 1,440; 1,468; 1,575; 4,725
9. 2,772; 2,976; 1,236; 2,568
10. 3,535; 2,097; 2,110; 6,560

Page 50
1. 144 pounds of grass seed
2. 235 tomato plants
3. 102 gallons
4. 92 bags of fertilizer
5. 115 lawns
6. 111 garden tools
7. 354 squash

Page 51
1. 44 rabbits
2. 84 red pet collars
3. 42 lettuce leaves
4. 39 poodles
5. 48 bags of seed
6. 96 times
7. 69 dog toys

Page 52
1. 44
2. 0
3. 32
4. 288
5. 396
6. 960

Page 53
1. 7,578 pages
2. 2,296 people
3. 4,752 magazines
4. 1,401 books
5. 2,848 books

Page 54
1. $10.26
2. 3,470¢ or $34.70
3. $116.62
4. 13,964¢ or $139.64
5. $8.15
6. $413.37

Page 55
1. 252 cupcakes
2. 2,443¢ or $24.43
3. 84 cans of soda
4. $41.97
5. 396 party hats
6. 224 inches of ribbon

Page 56
1. 0, 2, 4, 6, 8, 10, 12, 14, 16, 18, 20, 22, 24
2. 24, 22, 20, 18, 16, 14, 12, 10, 8, 6, 4, 2, 0
3. 14, 10, 2, 24, 18, 4, 8, 22, 12, 16, 0, 6, 20

Page 57
1. 0, 3, 6, 9, 12, 15, 18, 21, 24, 27, 30, 33, 36
2. 36, 33, 30, 27, 24, 21, 18, 15, 12, 9, 6, 3, 0
3. 21, 15, 3, 36, 27, 6, 12, 33, 18, 24, 0, 9, 30

Page 58
1. 0, 4, 8, 12, 16, 20, 24, 28, 32, 36, 40, 44, 48
2. 48, 44, 40, 36, 32, 28, 24, 20, 16, 12, 8, 4, 0
3. 28, 20, 4, 48, 36, 8, 16, 44, 24, 32, 0, 12, 40

Page 59
1. 0, 5, 10, 15, 20, 25, 30, 35, 40, 45, 50, 55, 60
2. 60, 55, 50, 45, 40, 35, 30, 25, 20, 15, 10, 5, 0
3. 35, 25, 5, 60, 45, 10, 20, 55, 30, 40, 0, 15, 50

Answer Pages

Page 60

1. 0, 6, 12, 18, 24, 30, 36, 42, 48, 54, 60, 66, 73

2. 73, 66, 60, 54, 48, 42, 36, 30, 24, 18, 12, 6, 0

3. 42, 30, 6, 72, 54, 12, 24, 66, 36, 48, 0, 18, 60

Page 61

1. 0, 7, 14, 21, 28, 35, 42, 49, 56, 63, 70, 77, 84

2. 84, 77, 70, 63, 56, 49, 42, 35, 28, 21, 14, 7, 0

3. 49, 35, 7, 84, 63, 14, 28, 77, 42, 54, 0, 21, 70

Page 62

1. 0, 8, 16, 24, 32, 40, 48, 56, 64, 72, 80, 88, 96

2. 96, 88, 80, 72, 64, 56, 48, 40, 32, 24, 16, 8, 0

3. 56, 40, 8, 96, 72, 16, 32, 88, 48, 64, 0, 24, 80

Page 63

1. 0, 9, 18, 27, 36, 45, 54, 63, 72, 81, 90, 99, 108

2. 108, 99, 90, 81, 72, 63, 54, 45, 36, 27, 18, 9, 0

3. 63, 45, 9, 108, 81, 18, 36, 99, 54, 72, 0, 27, 90

Page 64

1. 0, 10, 20, 30, 40, 50, 60, 70, 80, 90, 100, 110, 120

2. 120, 110, 100, 90, 80, 70, 60, 50, 40, 30, 20, 10, 0

3. 70, 50, 10, 120, 90, 20, 40, 110, 60, 80, 0, 30, 100

Page 65

1. 0, 11, 22, 33, 44, 55, 66, 77, 88, 99, 110, 121, 132

2. 132, 121, 110, 99, 88, 77, 66, 55, 44, 33, 22, 11, 0

3. 77, 55, 11, 132, 99, 22, 44, 121, 66, 88, 0, 33, 110

Page 66

1. 0, 12, 24, 36, 48, 60, 72, 84, 96, 108, 120, 132, 144

2. 144, 132, 120, 108, 96, 84, 72, 60, 48, 36, 24, 12, 0

3. 84, 60, 12, 144, 108, 24, 48, 132, 72, 96, 0, 36, 120

Page 67

top: 2,079; 6,732; 1,362
middle: 398; 2,720; 1,470
bottom: 3,996; 6,584; 1,494

Page 68

1. Lori
2. Tanner
3. Grayson

Page 69

2x2=4; 4x5=20; 20x7=140; 140x3=420; 402x6=2520

Page 70

3, 15, 13, 5;   come
20, 15;   to
13, 25;   my
8, 15, 21, 19, 5;   house
20, 15, 4, 1, 25;   today

Page 71–72

3 weeks x 3 days a week = 9 feedings

Page 73

24, milk
45, flour
54, sugar
15, eggs
42, butter

Page 74

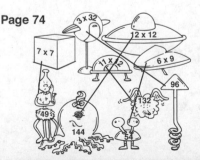